CONTENTS

IN SPACE

The Space Age began on 4th October 1957, when the first **satellite**, **Sputnik 1**, was sent into space. A satellite is a kind of spacecraft that travels around the Earth or other planets. Some spacecraft are manned – they have people inside. Others, such as satellites, are unmanned. Some satellites take photographs of Earth. Others send television pictures and telephone messages to different parts of the Earth. Scientists use satellites to study the Earth and the rest of the **universe**.

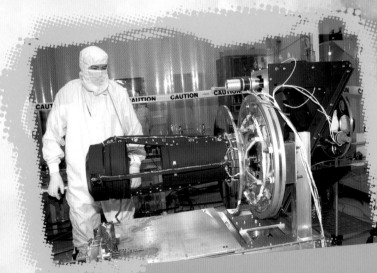

▲ The people who build spacecraft often wear overalls, hoods, gloves and even masks like surgeons in an operating room.

BUILDING SPACECRAFT

Spacecraft are built in workshops called clean rooms. The rooms have to be completely clean, because dust, oil and moisture can damage parts of a spacecraft.

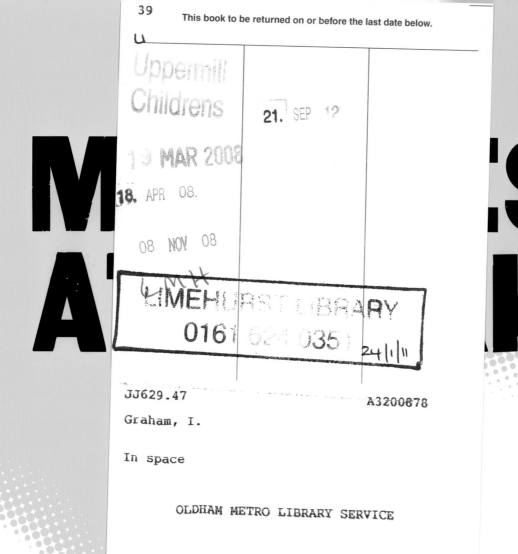

OLDHAM METRO LIBRARY SERVICE

IAN GRAHAM

QED Publishing

Written by Ian Graham
Produced by Calcium
Editor Sarah Medina
Foldout illustration by Ian Naylor
Picture Researcher Maria Joannou

Publisher Steve Evans
Creative Director Zeta Davies
Senior Editor Hannah Ray

Printed and bound in China

Words in **bold** can be found in the Glossary on page 34.

▼ The Space Shuttle blasts off on a mission to orbit the Earth. Unlike satellites and space probes, it is a manned spacecraft.

Exploring space

Space probes are used to explore the **solar system**. They are sent out from Earth to photograph planets and their **moons**. They make maps and take lots of measurements for scientists. A few space probes have landed on the **Moon** or on a planet so they can study its surface and **atmosphere**.

▼ Some planets are so far away, it can take years for a space probe to reach them.

FACT!
The Cassini space probe spent seven years flying from Earth to the planet Saturn.

EARTH SATELLITES

There are about 2500 satellites flying around the Earth. The path of a satellite around a planet is called an orbit. Some satellites circle the Earth from north to south, over the North **Pole** and the South Pole. Other satellites circle the middle of the Earth, around the **equator**. Some satellites take exactly one day to fly around the middle of the Earth. The Earth spins once a day too, so these satellites stay above the same spot on the ground all the time.

▲ **Communications** satellites receive signals from one part of the Earth and send them down to another part of the Earth.

FACT!
On 6 October 1959, Explorer 6 was the first satellite to send back a photograph of the Earth.

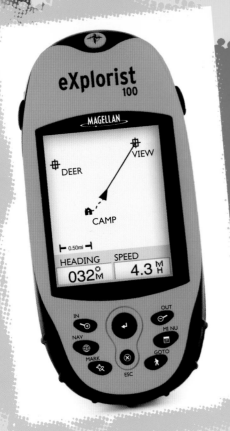

WHERE AM I?

Navigation satellites can tell you exactly where you are on the Earth. They are very useful if you are travelling somewhere or if you are lost. The Global Positioning System (GPS) has 24 navigation satellites. A GPS receiver on the ground works out where it is by measuring how long it takes for radio signals from the satellites to travel to the receiver.

◄ This little receiver uses radio signals from three GPS satellites in space to work out its position anywhere on Earth.

Space talk

The American space agency, **NASA**, has its own communications satellites in orbit above the Earth. They are called Tracking and Data Relay Satellites (TDRS). The TDR satellites receive signals from NASA, on Earth, and pass them on to spacecraft. The satellites also send signals from the spacecraft back to Earth. This means that NASA can send and receive all the information it needs 24 hours a day.

NASA's Tracking and Data Relay ► Satellites send radio signals between spacecraft and their controllers on Earth.

Space probes are unmanned spacecraft sent from Earth to study planets, moons, **comets** and **asteroids**. Scientists are interested in comets and asteroids because they are made of very old material that has not changed since the solar system began about 4.6 **billion** years ago. Space probes have flown past, orbited or landed on nearly every planet in the solar system.

Probing Eros

In 2000, the NEAR-Shoemaker space probe went into orbit around an asteroid called 433 Eros. NEAR-Shoemaker spent a year studying the asteroid and photographing it from as close as 5km away. Then its controllers on Earth did something the spacecraft wasn't designed to do. They landed the space probe on the asteroid!

▼ The large radio dish in the middle of NEAR–Shoemaker's **solar panels** receives instructions from Earth and sends information back to Earth.

SWEEPING DUST

The probe Stardust is an amazing spacecraft. It flew 3.2 billion kilometres to collect dust coming off a comet called Wild-2. Then it brought the dust back to Earth for scientists to study. Stardust also took close-up photographs of the comet as it flew by.

▲ The Stardust spacecraft approaches the dust cloud trailing behind comet Wild-2.

◄ These pictures show how the Rosetta space probe will swoop over comet 67P/Churyumov-Gerasimenko in 2014.

FACT!

The Voyager 1 space probe is the furthest man-made object from Earth. It is 14.7 billion kilometres away. This is much further away than the planets.

9

ORBITERS

Orbiters are space probes that orbit (fly around) the planets they study. To save fuel during the long journey through space, these probes use the pull of **gravity** of planets they pass to hurl them onwards. Then they fire a **rocket** engine to slow down just enough to go into orbit around the planet they have been sent to study. As the space probe circles the planet, its cameras and other instruments study the surface.

Venus Express

On 9th November 2005, the European Space Agency launched a spacecraft called Venus Express. It was sent to the planet Venus to study its atmosphere and to find out if volcanoes are still erupting on the planet's surface. The spacecraft's instruments can see right through Venus's thick atmosphere to its surface.

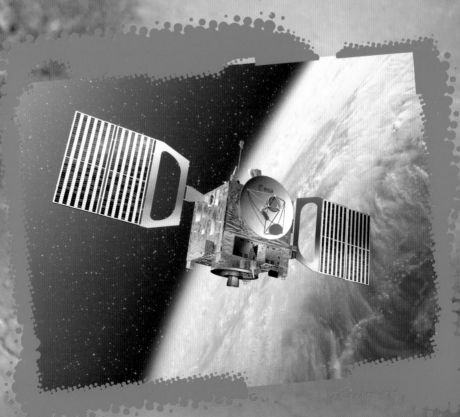

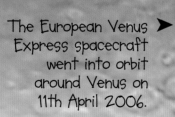

The European Venus ➤ Express spacecraft went into orbit around Venus on 11th April 2006.

GOING TO SATURN

In 2004, the Cassini spacecraft went into orbit around Saturn. The planet Saturn has huge rings around it and 56 moons. Cassini dropped a mini-probe called Huygens onto Titan, one of Saturn's moons. Huygens photographed Titan's surface. Scientists are very interested in Titan because, unlike most moons, it has an atmosphere.

Flight mechanics get the huge Cassini ➤ spacecraft ready for launch. The gold bowl on its side contains the Huygens mini-probe.

solar panel

radio dish

◄ In March 2006, seven months after it was launched, the Mars Reconnaissance Orbiter spacecraft began orbiting Mars.

FACT!
Cassini is the biggest spacecraft ever sent to explore a planet and its moons.

SPACE SHUTTLE

The Space Shuttle is the first manned spacecraft that can be used over and over again. It is made up of a fuel tank and two **boosters**, which carry an Orbiter into space. The Orbiter has a huge **payload bay** for carrying satellites, space laboratories and scientific experiments. It spends up to a month in space before it returns to Earth. Five Orbiters were built: Columbia, Challenger, Discovery, Atlantis and Endeavour.

▼ The Space Shuttle Orbiter has room for a crew of up to seven astronauts.

payload bay

FACT!
The Space Shuttle Orbiter **re-enters** the atmosphere at 25 times the speed of sound!

Lift-off

To launch the Space Shuttle, a huge fuel tank and two **solid rocket boosters** are needed. The tank holds fuel for the three rocket engines in the Orbiter's tail. The boosters provide most of the power for lift-off. The fuel tank and boosters fall back to Earth when their job is done.

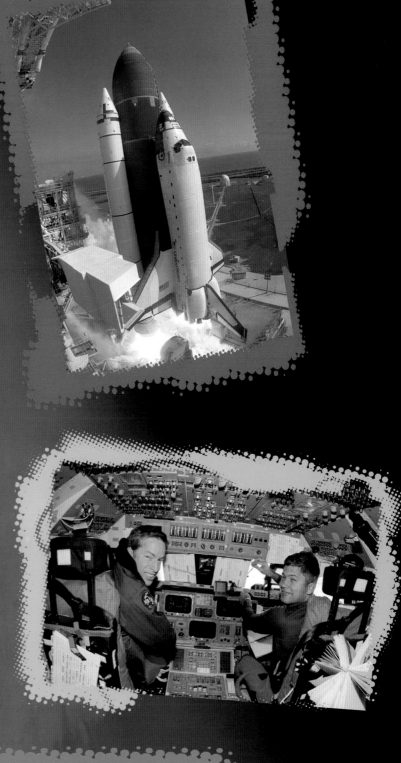

The Space Shuttle blasts off. You can ➤ see the orange fuel tank, one of the two white solid rocket boosters and the Orbiter.

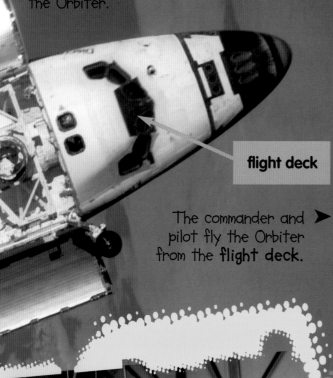

flight deck

The commander and ➤ pilot fly the Orbiter from the **flight deck**.

VIRTUAL REALITY

One way for an astronaut to train for a spaceflight is to use virtual reality. Goggles connected to a computer show the astronaut what he will see during a real spaceflight. The astronaut uses special gloves to pick things up and move them around, even though they aren't really there!

◀ Astronauts can train for a Space Shuttle mission using a virtual reality system. It works a bit like a computer game.

13

SOYUZ

Russian Soyuz spacecraft have been carrying people into space since 1967. The latest version, the Soyuz TMA, takes astronauts to the **International Space Station**, 400km above the Earth. Soyuz TMA has three parts, or **modules**, that link together. The service and orbital modules are at either end of the spacecraft. Between them is the re-entry module, which brings the astronauts home.

orbital module

A Soyuz spacecraft about to **dock** ➤ with the International Space Station.

▲ With three astronauts in their bulky spacesuits, there is not much room to spare inside the Soyuz re-entry module.

Flying Soyuz

Soyuz carries three astronauts in its re-entry module. They lie back on beds to make lift-off and landing more comfortable. Each bed is covered with a liner that is the same shape as the astronaut's body. The controls and computer screens for flying Soyuz are opposite the astronauts.

re-entry module

FACT!
The new Soyuz TMA spacecraft was designed to have more room inside for taller astronauts.

СОЮЗ

service module

LANDING

At the end of a spaceflight, the re-entry module separates from the other two modules. As it falls back into the Earth's atmosphere, a heat shield **protects the module from the fiery heat of re-entry.** Then parachutes open and slow it down. **Just before the module hits the ground, rockets fire to soften the landing.**

▲ The re-entry module of a Soyuz spacecraft lies on its side after returning from space.

15

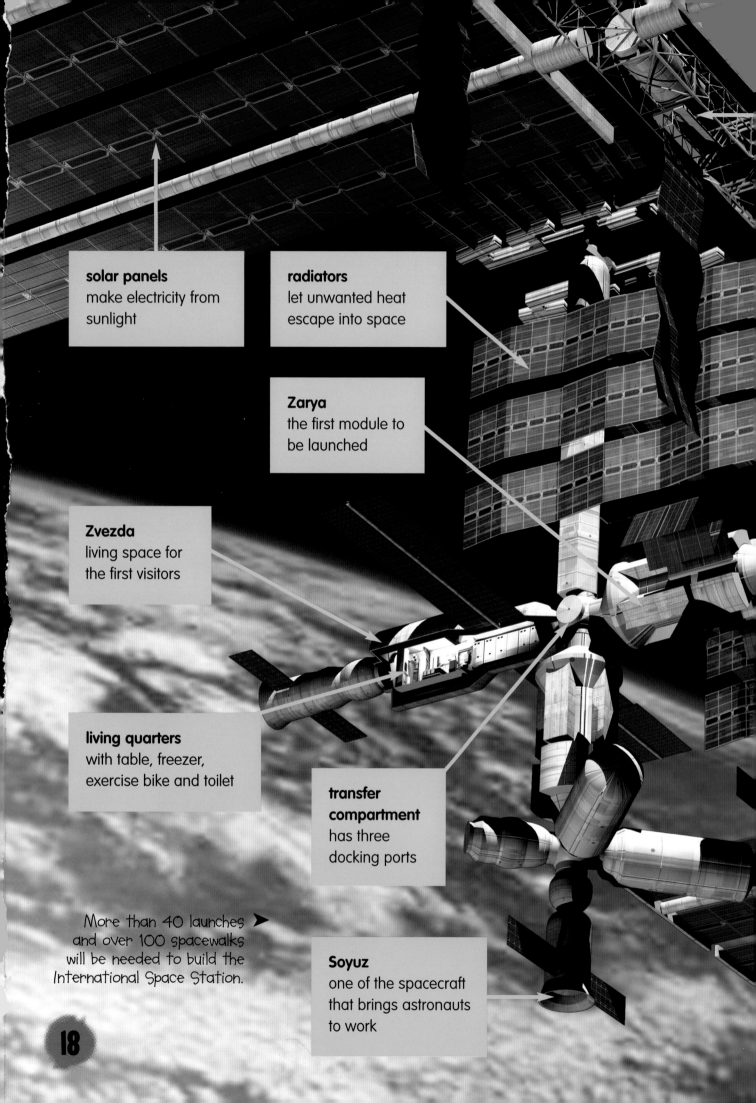

solar panels
make electricity from
sunlight

radiators
let unwanted heat
escape into space

Zarya
the first module to
be launched

Zvezda
living space for
the first visitors

living quarters
with table, freezer,
exercise bike and toilet

**transfer
compartment**
has three
docking ports

More than 40 launches ➤
and over 100 spacewalks
will be needed to build the
International Space Station.

Soyuz
one of the spacecraft
that brings astronauts
to work

International Space Station

Sixteen countries are working together to build the International Space Station (ISS), about 400km above the Earth. Like Mir, the ISS is too big and heavy to be launched in one piece. When the ISS is finished, it will measure 110m from end to end, and will weigh about 450 tonnes. It has a laboratory for doing scientific research. A crew of up to seven astronauts will run the station, with the help of 52 computers.

▲ These modules are being built for the International Space Station.

Construction

The parts of the International Space Station that people will live and work in are big metal tubes. They are made from a very light metal called aluminium. Connections called **docking ports** allow more modules to connect to the tubes. Visiting spacecraft can 'park' at these ports.

Sunrise

Russia started building the International Space Station when it launched the Zarya (Sunrise) module. Zarya is 12.5m long, 4m wide and weighs 20 tonnes. It has two rocket engines to boost the space station into a higher orbit, and 36 smaller jets to turn the station.

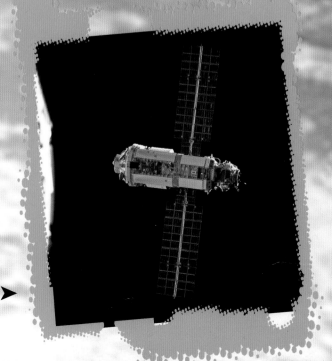

The Zarya module, built in Moscow, ▶ in Russia, was launched in 1998.

Most spacecraft stay in space for a few days or, occasionally, a couple of weeks before returning to Earth. **Space stations** are different. They stay in space for years, and crews take it in turns to run them. The first space stations were used to find out better ways to build, launch and run space stations. They also helped scientists to find out how astronauts are affected by long space flights. This research will help the scientists to design future missions to other planets.

Skylab

The American Skylab space station was made from rockets and spacecraft left over from the Apollo space missions, which landed astronauts on the Moon in the 1960s and 1970s. Skylab crews lived and worked inside part of a giant Saturn V moon-rocket. When Skylab was launched, it was shaken about so badly that one of its solar panels was torn off but, luckily, the space station survived.

▲ Skylab had more room inside than any other spacecraft.

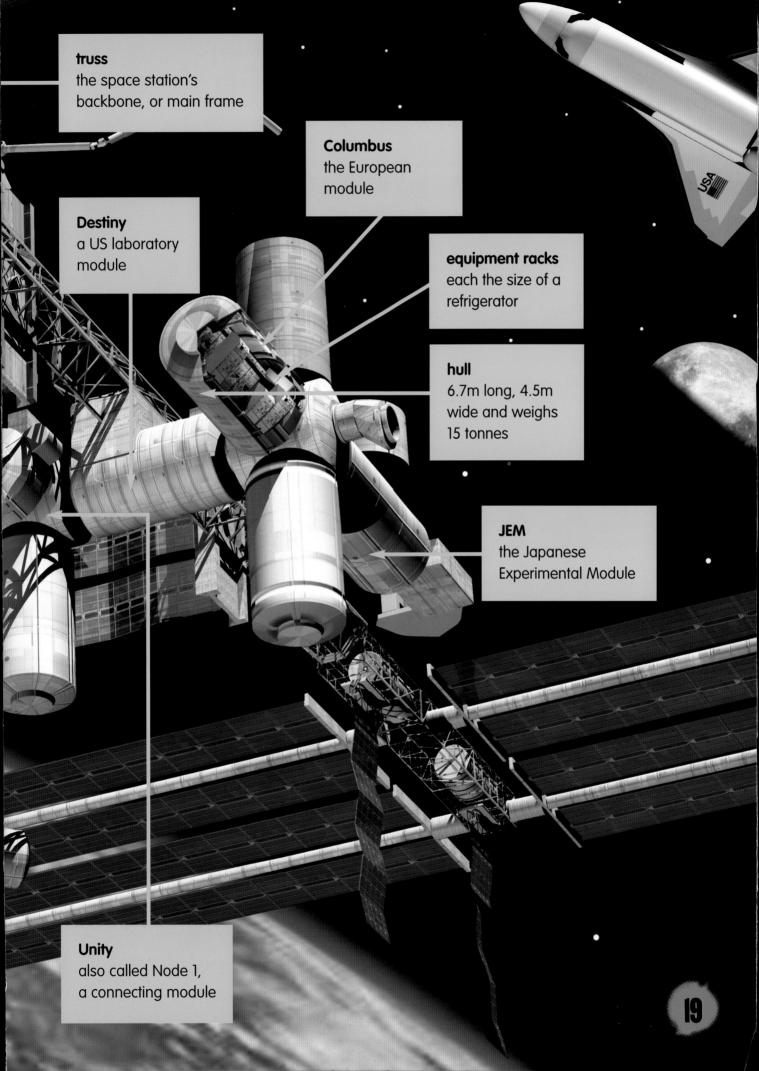

truss
the space station's backbone, or main frame

Columbus
the European module

Destiny
a US laboratory module

equipment racks
each the size of a refrigerator

hull
6.7m long, 4.5m wide and weighs 15 tonnes

JEM
the Japanese Experimental Module

Unity
also called Node 1, a connecting module

SPACESUITS

When astronauts have to leave the safety of their spacecraft and go outside, they wear a spacesuit to protect themselves. The spacesuit's backpack has everything the astronaut needs, including oxygen to breathe and radio communication. Astronauts heat up quickly inside their suits when they are working hard. The backpack can pump cool water through one of the spacesuit's layers to cool an astronaut down.

With a spacesuit and a backpack, ➤ an astronaut can work in space for several hours.

SAFER jetpack

A SAFER suit

During spacewalks, astronauts are tied to their spacecraft by a safety line called a tether. This line stops them from floating away into space. An astronaut also wears a jetpack, in case the tether snaps. This jetpack is called a Simplified Aid For **EVA** Rescue (SAFER). Jets of gas from a SAFER pack fly the astronaut back to the spacecraft.

▲ Astronauts who drift away can fire their SAFER jetpack to get back to their spacecraft.

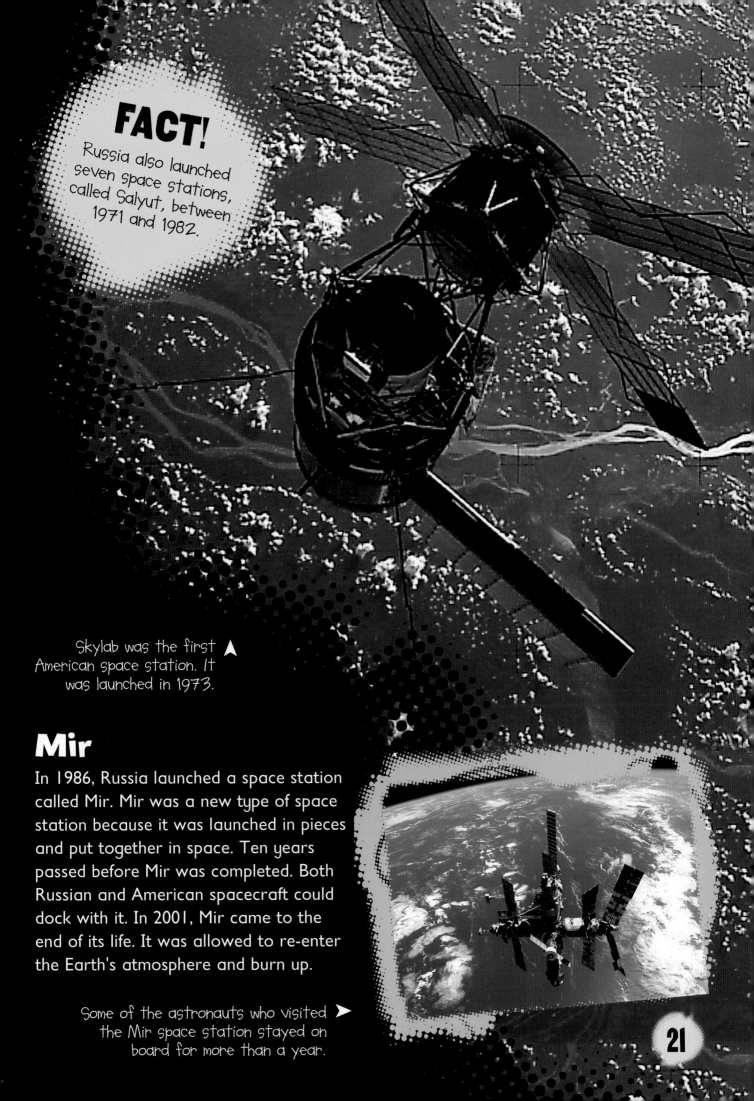

FACT!
Russia also launched
seven space stations,
called Salyut, between
1971 and 1982.

Skylab was the first ▲
American space station. It
was launched in 1973.

Mir

In 1986, Russia launched a space station
called Mir. Mir was a new type of space
station because it was launched in pieces
and put together in space. Ten years
passed before Mir was completed. Both
Russian and American spacecraft could
dock with it. In 2001, Mir came to the
end of its life. It was allowed to re-enter
the Earth's atmosphere and burn up.

Some of the astronauts who visited ➤
the Mir space station stayed on
board for more than a year.

COLUMBUS

The European Columbus module for the ISS is a science laboratory where astronauts will carry out research. The equipment needed for the experiments will be stored in ten racks. The racks are all the same size and shape, so the equipment for new experiments will slot in easily.

The Columbus orbiting laboratory is being ▲ built by 41 companies in 14 countries.

Delivering cargo

Europe is providing a cargo craft for the ISS, called the Automated Transfer Vehicle (ATV). It is also known as Jules Verne, after an author who wrote many exciting science fiction books. The ATV will carry supplies to the space station, but it does not need a crew to fly it. The ATV can find the space station and dock with it automatically.

◄ A Jules Verne cargo craft approaches the International Space Station.

▲ Training for spacewalks is done under water in one of the world's biggest swimming pools.

MEGA-MODELS

Life-size models of parts of the International Space Station and the Space Shuttle are used to train astronauts for spacewalks. They train under water wearing their spacesuits, because this feels very similar to being weightless in space.

FACT!

Each Space Shuttle spacesuit costs about £6.5 million!

AT THE LAUNCH PAD

Huge machines are needed to move spacecraft and to get them ready for lift-off. NASA's **crawler-transporters** were originally built to carry the giant Saturn V moon-rockets to the **launch pad** from the building where they were put together. Today, they do the same job for the Space Shuttle. The Space Shuttle and its launch platform weigh more than 6000 tonnes. A crawler-transporter has to carry them a distance of 6km to the launch pad.

NASA has two of these massive crawler-transporters. ▼

crawler-transporter

Shuttle launch pad

The Space Shuttle launch pad is a complicated machine. When the Shuttle is on the launch pad, a huge Rotating Service Structure (RSS) swings around it. It covers the spacecraft's payload bay, so that cargo can be loaded under cover. The RSS swings back out of the way before the launch.

▲ The Space Shuttle arrives at the launch pad. The Rotating Service Structure is out of the way, on the left.

Sea launch

Sometimes, satellites are launched from the sea. A Sea Launch rocket can carry a satellite weighing more than 6 tonnes. The Sea Launch and its command ship collect rockets and satellites from California, USA, and then sail to a spot near Christmas Island in the Pacific Ocean. This is where the launch takes place.

mobile launch platform

FACT!
When NASA's crawler-transporters were built in 1960, they were the world's largest tracked vehicles.

▲ A Sea Launch rocket blasts off carrying a satellite into orbit.

ROVERS

Rovers are robotic space vehicles that land on other planets or moons to explore the surface. They are controlled by drivers on Earth, but sometimes they don't follow orders! Radio signals take so long to travel from Earth to Mars that a rover could crash into a rock long before its driver could steer it to safety. Mars Exploration Rovers have been designed to work out when they are in danger and to steer around the problem.

cameras

radio antenna

➤ Two of these wheelbarrow-sized rovers landed on Mars in 2004.

FACT!
Mars rovers have heaters to stop them from freezing during the Martian night.

instrument arm

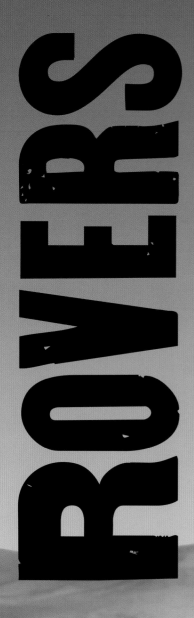

Mars Rovers

In 2004, two Mars Exploration Rovers, called Spirit and Opportunity, were sent to study Mars. On the journey, each rover was folded up inside a **lander** craft. Once on Mars, they unfolded and started exploring the planet's surface. **Solar cells** on top of the rovers made electricity for their motors and instruments. A mechanical arm at the front of each rover stretched out to study nearby rocks.

▲ Technicians check out a Mars Exploration Rover, which is folded up inside the open 'petals' of its lander craft.

A Mars lander craft, with its ➤ rover safely packed inside, fires rockets to soften its landing.

solar panel

VISITING MARS

After a rover dives into the Martian atmosphere from space, airbags blow up all around it like balloons. A parachute and rockets slow it down as the rover falls towards the surface. When it lands, the rover bounces and rolls to a stop. Then the airbags collapse and the lander craft opens.

ROCKETS

Spacecraft are launched by rockets. Rockets are powerful enough to lift heavy spacecraft and, unlike engines, they work in space. Engines need air to work but there is no air in space. The biggest rockets are made up of two or three smaller rockets standing on top of each other. These smaller rockets are called **stages**. When each stage has used up all of its fuel, it falls away. This makes the rest of the rocket lighter, so it can soar away even faster.

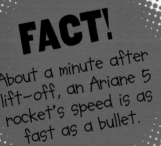

FACT!
About a minute after lift-off, an Ariane 5 rocket's speed is as fast as a bullet.

▲ Ariane 5 rockets are launched from the European Space Agency's Spaceport in French Guiana, in South America.

Ariane 5

Ariane 5, which made its first successful flight in 1997, is Europe's most powerful rocket. It is made from two booster rockets, strapped to a two-stage rocket in the middle. The boosters provide most of the **thrust** needed to launch the 780-tonne rocket into space.

◄ An Ariane 5 rocket stands on the launch pad during the final **countdown** to the launch.

▼ A Proton rocket blasts off. One of these rockets launched the first part of the International Space Station.

Proton

Proton is a Russian rocket with the fire power to launch the heaviest payloads. Five-tonne space probes can be launched to other planets by Proton. It can also take satellites and parts of space stations that weigh up to four times this much into orbit around the Earth.

29

SPACE SCOPES

Scientists learn about **stars** by studying the energy they give out. The swirling air in the Earth's atmosphere makes stars twinkle and stops **telescopes** on Earth from taking clear pictures of them. Stars give out more energy than just light, but the Earth's atmosphere blocks a lot of this invisible energy, too. Space telescopes in orbit above the atmosphere receive all the energy given out by stars, and take better pictures.

▲ The Hubble Space Telescope orbits the Earth 610km above the ground.

FACT!

The Hubble Space Telescope has made more than 400 000 observations of 25 000 objects.

Hubble Space Telescope

The Hubble Space Telescope was launched from the Space Shuttle in 1990. The Hubble can see objects in space that are 50 times fainter than anything that can be seen by telescopes on Earth. It takes clear pictures and sends them back to Earth by radio.

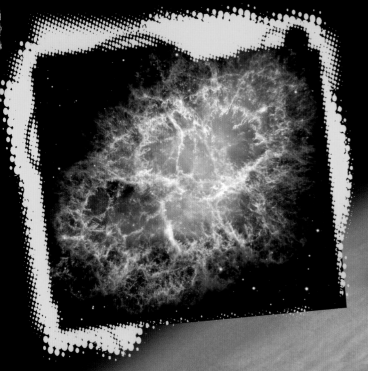

▲ The Hubble Space Telescope took this picture of the Crab **Nebula**. This is a star that exploded nearly 1000 years ago.

▼ The James Webb Space Telescope will see objects that are 400 times fainter than anything that can be seen by telescopes on the Earth's surface.

SON OF HUBBLE

The Hubble Space Telescope is nearing the end of its working life. It will be replaced by an even bigger telescope called the James Webb Space Telescope. This is due to be launched in about the year 2013. It will study the birth of new planets, stars and galaxies.

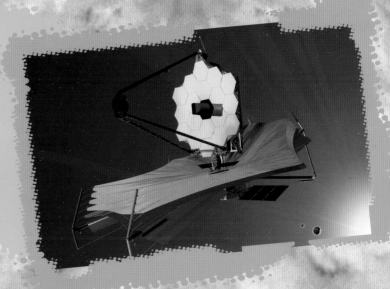

Heat scope

The Spitzer Space Telescope is an **infrared** telescope. It studies the heat given out by objects in space. This lets it look through clouds of gas and dust, and see whatever is hidden inside or behind them. **Astronomers** are interested in these hidden areas of space because they are where new stars form.

◄ The Spitzer Space Telescope makes pictures from heat instead of light.

SPACESHIPONE

Until recently, all spacecraft were launched by space agencies that have government help, such as NASA. The Ansari X Prize offered a reward of US$10 million to the first organization to launch a manned spacecraft without any help from government. To win the prize, the spacecraft had to be launched into space twice within two weeks. Twenty-six teams took part in the race. In 2004, a spaceplane called SpaceShipOne was declared the winner.

At the controls

SpaceShipOne's pilot sits in a cockpit like an aircraft cockpit. He breathes through a mask, and wears a helmet and a flight suit. He also wears a parachute in case he has to jump out in an emergency.

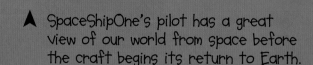

▲ SpaceShipOne's pilot has a great view of our world from space before the craft begins its return to Earth.

jet engine

White Knight
cockpit

SpaceShipOne

◄ SpaceShipOne is launched from underneath a specially built aircraft at a height of 15km above the ground.

COMING HOME

When SpaceShipOne has gone as high as it can, its two tails swivel upwards. This shape slows the spaceplane down to a safe speed as it falls back into the atmosphere. SpaceShipOne is the first craft to use this way of re-entering the atmosphere. Then it glides down and lands on a runway.

nose skid

wheels

▲ Just before SpaceShipOne lands, the pilot lowers the wheels and a nose skid.

GLOSSARY

asteroid an object made of rock, smaller than a planet, that orbits the Sun

astronomer a scientist who studies the stars, planets and other objects in space

atmosphere the air that surrounds the Earth, or the gases that surround other planets or moons

billion one thousand million

booster a rocket that provides extra power to help a bigger rocket take off

comet a ball of rock, dust and ice in orbit around the Sun

communicate to pass on or share information

countdown the time, counted backwards to zero, leading to the launch of a rocket

crawler-transporters giant vehicles used at the Kennedy Space Centre in Florida, USA, for carrying Space Shuttles from the place where they are built to the launch-pad where they take off

dock to link up with a spacecraft. Spacecraft dock by locking themselves together

docking port the part on a spacecraft where another craft can lock onto it. Hatches (doors) in the ports open after docking to let astronauts go through

equator an imaginary line around the Earth midway between the North and South Poles

EVA extra-vehicular activity, another name for a spacewalk

flight deck the part of an aeroplane or Space Shuttle where the pilots sit and control the craft

gravity the force that pulls objects towards each other because of the matter they are made of. Gravity stops everything flying off the Earth into space and it holds the planets in their orbits around the Sun

heat shield part of a spacecraft designed to protect it from the intense heat caused by entering an atmosphere at high speed from space

infrared a type of invisible energy, like light, but made of longer waves that we cannot see. Hot objects give out infrared waves

International Space Station a large spacecraft being built in Earth's orbit. It is being built by 16 countries and involves over 100 000 people

lander a spacecraft, or part of a spacecraft, that lands on another planet or moon

launch pad a platform from which a rocket takes off

module a section or compartment of a spacecraft that can be detached from the rest of the spacecraft

Moon the Earth's only natural satellite

moon a natural satellite orbiting a planet

NASA the US National Aeronautics and Space Administration. NASA is the organization in charge of American spaceflights

nebula a vast cloud of dust or gas in space

payload bay the part of the Space Shuttle Orbiter where cargo is carried

34

pole the farthest point either north (North Pole) or south (South Pole) of the Earth's equator

re-entry coming back into the Earth's atmosphere from space

receiver a radio that takes in, or receives, radio signals

rocket a type of engine with its own supply of fuel as well as the oxygen needed to burn the fuel. Rockets are extremely powerful and they can work in space where there is no air

satellite a smaller object orbiting a larger object. A moon is a natural satellite of a planet. A spacecraft in orbit around a planet is an artificial satellite

solar cell an electronic device that changes sunlight into electricity. A sheet of solar cells is also called a solar panel

solar panel part of a satellite or space probe that makes electricity from sunlight using solar cells

solar system the Sun and all the planets, moons, comets, asteroids, dust and gas that orbit it

solid rocket booster a rocket that burns solid fuel to give a bigger rocket or space vehicle extra power for take-off

space probe an unmanned spacecraft that explores space and sends information back to Earth

Space Shuttle a rocket-powered space vehicle that can travel into space again and again

space station a large spacecraft that stays in space for months or years and is visited by a series of crews

Sputnik I the first satellite ever launched from Earth, in 1957. Sputnik is a Russian word meaning 'travelling companion'

stage part of a rocket with its own engine and fuel. When one stage has used up all of its fuel, it falls away and the next stage takes over

star an object in the sky that is far bigger than any planet. Stars give out light and heat

telescope an instrument for studying distant objects in space

thrust the force produced by a rocket engine

universe everything that exists, including the Earth, stars and planets

FIND OUT MORE

Websites

For fun space-related games, activities and facts:
http://spaceplace.jpl.nasa.gov/en/kids

Find out about spacesuits, spacecraft and living in space:
http://www.esa.int/esaKIDSen

Find out where the International Space Station is right now:
http://spaceflight.nasa.gov/realdata/tracking

Read about the International Space Station:
http://school.discovery.com/schooladventures/spacestation

INDEX